Canterbury

in old picture postcards

by
Terry Hougham

Terry Hougham

European Library - Zaltbommel/Netherlands MCMLXXXVII

About the author
All the illustrations shown in this book are actual postcards from the authors own extensive collection. Terry Hougham has been a post-card collector since the 1950s and with the revival of the 'Golden Age' of deltiology in the last ten years, he has helped foster the interest in this hobby. With his enthusiasm and that of several other local collectors, the Canterbury and East Kent Postcard Club was founded in 1980.

Acknowledgements
I would like to thank my wife Anne, for the typing, correcting and retyping of this manuscript and for her tolerance in all the hours and days spent searching for these 'gems' of local history, at fairs and antique shops. I would also like to thank our good friends Colleen and Jim Howard for proof reading and correcting the text.

GB   ISBN 90 288 3424 9 / CIP

© 1987 European Library - Zaltbommel/Netherlands

European Library in Zaltbommel/Netherlands publishes among other things the following series:

IN OLD PICTURE POSTCARDS *is a series of books which sets out to show what a particular place looked like and what life was like in Victorian and Edwardian times. A book about virtually every town in the United Kingdom is to be published in this series. By the end of this year about 300 different volumes will have appeared. 1,500 books have already been published devoted to the Netherlands with the title* **In oude ansichten.** *In Germany, Austria and Switzerland 650, 100 and 25 books have been published as* **In alten Ansichten;** *in France by the name* **En cartes postales anciennes** *and in Belgium as* **In oude prentkaarten** *and/or* **En cartes postales anciennes** *150 respectively 400 volumes have been published.*

For further particulars about published or forthcoming books, apply to your bookseller or direct to the publisher.

This edition has been printed and bound by Grafisch Bedrijf De Steigerpoort in Zaltbommel/Netherlands.

INTRODUCTION

Every English City, whether old or new, has its own special claims to distinction, but Canterbury's appeal is universal. No other town in England can boast of more varied and historic associations from the earliest period of British history. Canterbury was a place of note during the early Roman occupation, Norman and Saxon remains are still being uncovered today by the archaelogical digs in and around the city. But it is the early Christianity attachment of Canterbury that attracts the modern day pilgrims to visit the magnificent Cathedral embracing every variety of English ecclesiastical architecture. Within the confines of this book it is only possible to scratch the surface of the history of the Mother Church and to quote from the great American Ambassador, the Hon. *Joseph Hodges Choate,* who declared: 'It is the bounden duty of every English speaking man and woman to visit Canterbury at least once in their lives.'

Canterbury is pleasantly situated in a valley surrounded by hills, with the river Stour meandering through the city, where it divides into two streams not far from each other. One runs through the Westgate Gardens and under the bridge at the Westgate and onto Barton, whilst the other flows past the Grey Friars, under the Kings Bridge and onto Blackfriars, uniting again and proceeding towards Fordwich. Numerous attempts have been made to render the river navigable, the last in 1825 but this failed, partly due to the introduction of the railway. The Canterbury and Whitstable Railway being opened on 3rd May 1830. At one time Canterbury had three main line stations: the South Eastern Railway Station with the line from Ashford to Thanet plus Whitstable Branch; The London, Chatham and Dover Station and the South Canterbury Station on the Elham Valley Line.

Years ago Canterbury was a walled in city with turretts or watch towers, several of which still exist. In the seventeenth century there were six gates as follows: *Newingate,* built in 1470 at the west end of St. George's Street and destroyed in 1801; *Burgate* at the east end of Burgate Street but taken down in 1822 to widen the street; *Northgate* on the road to Thanet, demolished in 1830; *Wincheap Gate,* built on the south side of the city to replace *Worthgate* but demolished in 1770; *Riding Gate* on the Dover Road, taken down in 1782, and *Westgate,* the only city gate which still remains, built in 1380 but in mid-Victorian times it was in imminent danger of destruction, under the pretext that 'its materials would provide excellent metal for the roads', fortunately the Westgate was saved.

Outside the city walls bounding the Dane John was part of the City Moat, now Rheims Way. Up until 1904 this remained as a 'Cabbage patch' when Councillor Bennett Goldney leased this land and transformed it into a pleasure ground, planting it with ornamental shrubs and trees and then opened it up to the public. At one end was a bowling green, the Capston from Nelson's flagship the *Foudroyant* found an honoured place, as did a Great War tank in 1919 and all around the city peacocks strutted and screamed, drawing attention to their brilliant plumage.

Charles Dickens, the great Victorian novelist and poet, has been closely identified with Broadstairs and Rochester but his associations with Canterbury are apt to be overlooked. Dickens loved this city and in several of his well-known books, scenes were drawn from here. In Sun Street, Mr. Micawber's Hotel, the Little Inn and in Chantry Lane, Uriah Heep's 'Ome were immortalised in David Copperfield. As was the old Cattle Market with Betsy Trotwood 'insinuating her grey pony among the carts baskets, vegetables and huckster's goods'. 'The hairbreath turns and twists we made, drew upon us a variety of speeches from the people standing about, but my Aunt drove on with perfect indifference.' An old house in Burgate, now the National Trust Shop, the interior of which is described as that of Mr. Wickfield's residence, whilst the House of Agnes lays claim to this also. Finally Dr. Strong's private residence was in Lady Wootton's Green where 'some of the higher scholars boarded' and where David became a frequent visitor.

The 16th century poet Christopher 'Kit' Marlowe was a native of the city, baptised in St. George's Church, he became a King's School scholar and thence to Cambridge for a Bachelors degree in 1583 and a Master's in 1587. In 1891 a bronze statue of a muse was erected in the Old Butter Market, to commemorate the tercentenary of the poet, but was moved slightly after a few years to give a better view of the fine old Christchurch Gate. In 1921 the statue was moved again, this time to the Dane John Gardens and replaced with a War Memorial.

Geoffrey Chaucer, one of the greatest names in English literature, was made famous through his 'Canterbury Tales'. The story evolves around a pilgrimage from London to Canterbury by thirty distinct figures, representing every class of English society from the Miller and his dogs, the Knight, the Wife of Bath, to the Ploughman, each with their own tales to relate. A famous painting completed in 1817 by Stothard 'The Pilgrims to Canterbury' is now owned by the Royal Museum.

Besides weaving, tannery, beer and mineral water's there were no large industries in Canterbury. During the religious persecutions in France and the Netherlands a large number of Huguenot refugees settled in the city and their craftsmen introduced weaving as an industrial pursuit. So successful did this industry become that over two thousand hand loom weavers were at one time employed but this was on the decline by the 1840s. After a lapse of years efforts were made in the early 1900s to revive hand weaving in the old house seen from the King's Bridge. A large mineral water trade was built up by people such as Sidney Holden of Longport, Edwin Bing at his shop in St. George's Street plus steam works in Monastery Street, and Miss Mary Ann Robins of Malvern House, Broad Street, the later being an example of womens liberation being established in 1865 and continuing until 1923.

The brewer's were Ash, Dane John Brewery; George Beer, Star Brewery Broad Street, and Flint's St. Dunstan's Brewery.

The vicinity of Canterbury is noted for its growth of hops, there being thousands of acres devoted to their cultivation affording employment for countless hands in the picking season. The railways put on special hopping trains to bring the poorer classes down from London to meet up with the local people and spend their annual holidays in the hop fields.

Photography was well-established by the 1890s, large brass cameras were mounted on cumbersome wooden tripods, the professionals peering out from a voluminous black cloth, recording accidents, events and life in general as they happened. Some of the local photographers were John Charlton, Arthur Colbourne, Henry Collis, Fisk-Moore, and Frank Bailey. With the advent of the postcards these photographs were produced as picture postcards and were for sale in the local shops sometimes within a day of the event. Fortunately such photographs were treasured in family albums and through this book it is hoped to share some of the pre-war life of Canterbury with you.

Canterbury Cathedral S. W

1. No book of Canterbury can be compiled without reference to the Cathedral. Probably the best overall view is taken from the Chistchurch Gate as this postcard published by J.G. Charlton shows. This magnificent gracefully sculptured Gothic stonework bearing the impress of centuries, its splended beauty of Bell Harry Tower soaring heavenwards, the city's 'crowning glory' must stand supreme. To chronicle a history of this imposing pinnacle of christianity would fill more than this book, but once inside the lure of its traditions will seize you as you stroll through the Crypt, stand by the Black Prince's tomb or approach the north-west transept, better known as the 'Martyrdom' where the murder of Archbishop Thomas à Becket took place in 1170. Wandering through the Cathedral past the Baptistry, Dark Entry, Green Court and Norman Staircase makes the pilgrim realise that its characteristics distinguish it from any other Cathedral in England, making it the 'Mother Church'.

2. There could be no better way to start a tour of Canterbury than by joining the waiting people on Tyler Hill Halt, just on the outskirts of Canterbury, for the Invicta Engine and carriage to arrive from Whitstable. The Canterbury and Whitstable Railway was opened on 3rd May 1830 and known locally as the 'Crab and Winkle' line. It was the first railway to employ steam power in southern England. In fact it was the first in the world to operate a steam passenger service, four miles of the journey being operated by a stationary steam winding engine and two miles by the 'Invicta' steam. Tyler Hill and Blean Halt was opened in 1908 and consisted of a low platform, two hundred feet long, lit by oil lamps hung on locomotive brackets fitted to wooden posts. The halt keeper issued and collected tickets, managed the level crossing and lived in the nearby cottage, shown in the photograph taken about 1908. The Halt closed in January 1931 because it was some distance from Tyler Hill and Blean, the residents succumbed to the developing motor bus. The Tyler Hill site is now occupied by a private bungalow and the only trace of the railway is some timber boundary fence posts.

3. On the train journey into Canterbury West Station the line travels near the Canterbury Rifle Club's outdoor range and on 17th January 1907 the recently formed club with over one hunderd members had their new outdoor range formally declared open. Situated in Mr. Water Cozens sand pit adjacent to the tunnel on the Whitstable Railway the range had three firing distances: 25, 50 and 75 yards. A large number of people assembled in the afternoon to see the Mayor Bennet Goldney open the range and then using a rifle fitted with Morris tube and fire the first shot, which proved to be a bull. To the left of the picture can be seen another photographer recording the scene. Following this a rifle match took place between Colonel Thompson, Major Sparrow and Captain Whetherly of the 7th Dragoon Guards against the Mayor, Deputy Mayor Anderson and Sheriff Bourne, which proved successful for the military gentlemen by a comfortable margin of points.

4. This is a photograph of St. Stephen's Green, showing Ye Olde Beverlie which was originally built by Sir Roger Manwood, Baron of the Exchequer, about 1570 and adjoining a row of Alms houses. In 1629 the house was converted into an inn trading in Celebrated Ales and London Porter. In their tea garden adjoining, the Beverlie was one of the original inns where the old game of 'Bat and Trap' was played but it also has a long and historic association with cricket. The first game of cricket ever is believed to have been played on the Green immediately in front of the Beverlie, and Kent first played these as a County side. The photograph was taken in September 1907 when the public house was run by Mr. W. Banks, the Parish Clerk. To the left of the picture can be seen part of Hackington Council School run at this time by School Master and Mistress Mr. and Mrs. Matta and another postcards shows the school children in the playground dressed in smocks and knickerbockers.

CANTERBURY WEST STATION.

5. When the Southern Railways branch line from Ashford to Thanet reached Canterbury in 1846, the Canterbury and Whitstable line was diverted by a spur into the new station, later to be called Canterbury West. The postcard, showing the front entrance to the station with its attractive façade and Doric columns, was posted in 1906. One of the advertising signs was for Ash's Ales and Stout, Dane John Brewery. This imposing building stood in St. John's Lane, whilst another sign depicts the Orient Express. To the right of the picture can be seen two horse-drawn cabs plying for hire. During the 1920s a local character 'Blind Harry' stood for hours outside this station, tin mug in hand, held out, and bowler hat on his head. There was considerable confusion until after the turn of the century with three station roads in Canterbury, namely Station Road (S.E.R.), Station Road (L.C.D.R.) and Station Road. To clarify the position in 1904 they were re-named Station Road West, Station Road East and Station Road South.

6. The Cavalry Barracks, on the road out of Canterbury to Thanet, were built in 1794 to accommodate 2,000 Infantry and our picture shows the 7th (Princess Royal) Dragoon Guards, marching along Sturry Road, towards Northgate. Under the command of Colonel Dietz, the B & C companies left their barracks at 8 a.m. on Thursday 17th September 1908 and marched to Canterbury West Station. On arrival the men were 'formed up' outside the station, where a very large crowd had assembled to say farewell as the troops started their departure for Cairo, Egypt. The 7th Dragoon Guards had been quartered at Canterbury since 1904 and were thus taking fond memories of the city away with them, another two companies were leaving the following week. On the left hand side of Sturry Road can be seen part of the Barracks whilst to the right are the Vauxhall Tavern and Henry Attwood's General shop with the enamel signs for Lipton's Tea on the side of the house.

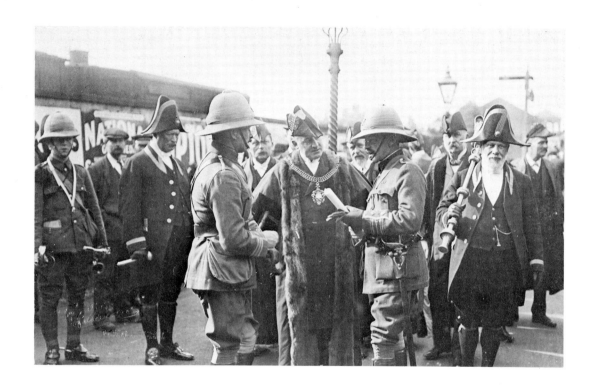

7. Continuing the story of the departure of the 7th Dragoon Guards, this postcards shows the platform of Canterbury West Station with General Fanshawe (Commanding the 2nd Calvalry Brigade), Colonel Dietz, the Mayor of Canterbury, Bennett Goldney, Alderman Mason, Sheriff Whittaker and several Councillors. The Mayor presented Colonel Dietz with a sealed letter of thanks from the Council for all the help the Guards had given the city. The postcard, published by Fisk Moore, photographer of St. George's Gate, was postmarked 24th September, one week after the event, part of the message reads: 'I will buy and send all nine cards.'

8. This photograph of St. Dunstan's Street, was taken from the Canterbury Baths on the corner of Station Road West (see card number 10) looking up towards the level crossing and Whitstable Road. Posted in March 1909, which must have been a very bad winter by the piles of snow in the view, part of the message reads '…thought you would like to have this postcard of our street to see the snows, hope you are keeping well this snowy weather. We have had such alot more'. There is a distinct lack of traffic in this normally busy road, one pony and trap can be seen at the level crossing gate and even pedestrians are not much in evidence. To the left of the street is shown part of the Rose and Crown public house, followed by C. David's hairdressing shop, full of tobacco advertisements and next to the House of Agnes Hotel. Whilst on the other side can be seen G.H. Teal, corn and seed merchants' shop with the Salvation Army's Divisional Headquarters above. During Cricket Week Mr. David used to run a popular service by exhibiting the latest Kent cricket scores in his shop window.

Level Crossing St Dunstans

9. This photograph was taken from the Hanover Place turning, but because of the association with Germany was re-named Roper Road at the beginning of the First World War. Charles William Allen, one of Canterbury's early photographers from the 1880s, lived at No. 1 Hanover Place and traded from the Westgate Studio, St. Dunstan's Street (between Kirby Lane and Station Road West). Mr. Allen was a councillor from 1885 and in 1888 filled the office of Sheriff, but died on the first day of 1889 when he was 62 years old. All his old photographs showed a superb vignette of the Westgate Towers on the back of each card. Looking down St. Dunstan's Street towards the level crossing and the Westgate Towers this picture shows Flint and Sons, Unicorn public house on the right. The photographer was very skillful to capture the South Eastern Locomotive, a Class 'B1' 4-4-0, as it puffed away from the station, over the level crossing towards Ashford.

Old Baths, Canterbury

62555

10. This picturesque old 15th century house stood in the parish of St. George's reputed to be the Old Toll House, at 3 Upper Bridge Street and was saved from destruction by the local patriotism of Mr. Walter Cozens, builder and decorator, who in 1906 had the old house taken down and re-erected in Station Road West. Built originally with its gables against the houses on each side, but in reconstruction the roof was placed the other way so that the gables could be seen from the street. For 2d you could visit the upper floor museum and collection of curios, local relics and old maps. Whilst the ground floor contained a swimming bath and several private rooms for warm baths at low charges, which must have been appreciated by both visitors and residents alike. In 1922 the house was turned into the old Canterbury House Café, specialities, delicious ices and chocolate could be bought there together with postcards as souvenirs but sad to say this house was bombed in the Second World War.

30   CANTERBURY. — The House of Agnes.

11. The House of Agnes at 71 St. Dunstan's Street with another in Burgate (mentioned in the preface) has long been traditionally associated with Charles Dickens. This remarkably fine old house in an excellent state of preservation, was believed to have been Mr. Wickfield's 'very old house bulging out still further, so that I fancied the whole house was leaning forward, trying to see who was passing on the narrow pavement below'. To the right of the building can be seen closed gates which lead to the old coaching shed and stables at the rear and it does not take much imagination to think back to the days when David Copperfield stayed here whilst going to school at Canterbury.

The Gateway, Roper House, Canterbury

12. Along the road from Hanover Place walking towards St. Dunstan's Church we come to the Old Tudor Gateway, which once formed the entrance to the imposing mansion of the Roper family. Margaret Roper, the daughter of St. Thomas More, resided there. The Tudor Gateway is all that remains of the estate which has long since been destroyed and at this time was used as the entrance to Flint and Sons, St. Dunstan's Brewery. Founded in 1797 the brewery's horse-drawn delivery drays were a well-known feature of Canterbury's streets. In about 1900 Mr. Sidney Harvey analytical chemist to the city reported upon samples of their finest Kentish Ales and Stout, which was bottled at the brewery, and stated 'I find them to be of first class quality, perfectly pure and sound in condition, evidently the products of the best Malt and Hops'. The brewery was finally taken over in 1924 by A. Leney and Co. Dover and then Fremlins Brothers two years later.

London Rd, Canterbury.

13. The most prominent feature of this postcard could have been St. Dunstan's Church, but as this has changed little since it was built, the road by the side of the church seemed a better picture. London Road with its trees on sentry duty on one side and cobble stones on the other has not changed very much either in over seventy years. On the right of the postcard was St. Dunstan's Nursery and with a 'glass' the following can be made out 'W.R. Pierce, Decorative Florist St. Duns...' To the right behind the trees is St. Dunstan's Church which was founded by Archbishop Lanfranc at the end of the 11th century. It was here that King Henry II changed his royal dress for that of a penitent, and walked 'barefoot and weeping' to perform his penance at the tomb of St. Thomas à Becket in the Cathedral Crypt. Under the Roper Chancel the head of Sir Thomas More was buried. He was beheaded on Tower Hill in 1535 because of his opposition to the divorce of Queen Catherine of Arragon from Henry VIII and the Kings marriage to Anne Boleyn. Margaret Roper, the oldest daughter of St. Thomas More, subsequently obtained possession of her father's head and brought it to Canterbury.

Cricket Week Illuminations St Dunstans Canterbury Aug. 1907.

14. Cricket Week is always the first week in August when visitors are attracted to the city by the thousand and for a short time Canterbury may be said to boast of a season equal to many fashionable watering places. The County Ground adjoins the Old Dover Road and the principal wicket is jealously guarded and carefully tended so that it will be as perfect as possible for 'That Week'. With a theme of 'Canterbury at Night' for 1907 the whole main streets were spanned with pretty coloured electric 'fairy' lamps, forming a beautiful arcade of lights. Besides this commencing at Station Road West and extending along the main thoroughfares to the end of St. George's Place at intervals of about twenty-five yards, festoons of small flags also spanned the roads. At the centre of each bunting Chinese lanterns were hung and Mercery Lane was decorated in the same charming manner, with baskets of flowers and Chinese lanterns. Not forgetting the Dane John Gardens entrance with its 'Welcome' sign and the bandstand (see cards 62-63): these were all very much part of the Cricket Festival.

19 CANTERBURY. — Westgate. L.L.

15. The most prominent feature after the Cathedral is the Westgate Towers, with its huge twin turrets, massive and magnificent, steeped in history since being entirely rebuilt by Archbishop Simon of Sudbury in 1380. To the left can be seen the old Falstaff Hotel, established in 1403, where pilgrims rested overnight when the Westgate closed after dusk. A few shops futher on can be seen the George and Dragon public house selling Ash's Ales from the Dane John Brewery, also Hadfield's bakeries daily delivery of bread by horse and cart. The Westgate was always used as the City's Gaol until 1829, a purpose for which it was not particularly well fitted owing to its lack of accommodation, but the prisoners however, never seem to have been numerous. Adjoining the gate in Pound Lane, the City Police Station was built and from then on used as a reception for criminals. The force also constituted a Fire Brigade, their large ladder being conveniently parked under the Towers. Until 1775 the Ground Floor Chamber in the South Tower contained a large circular iron cage in which debtors and other harmless prisoners were allowed to vary the prolonged monotany of their prison life by soliciting alms or food from a sympathetic public. In the lofty Guard Chamber over the archway the condemned cell may still be seen intact and the timbers of the gallows.

74 CANTERBURY.-Interior of Westgate Towers.-Shewing old Condemned Cell and Collection of Ancient Arms.-Also Machine Gun used by Kentish Yeomanry in Boer War.

16. The view of Canterbury and the Cathedral from the top of the Westgate Towers is most impressive, ascent being made by the winding stairs which are not unduly exhausting. Formally opened in June 1906 by the Mayor, the building now forms part of the Royal Museum. In the guard chamber could be seen a series of life size figures of medieval Knights and Barons. These figures were the original artist's models from which the statues were cast by Messrs. Elkington for the House of Lords. Also in this room was a collection of old guns, blunderbusses, flintlocks and a machine gun taken by the East Kent Company of the Imperial Yeomanry to South Africa for the Boer War and presented in 1907 by Lord Harris, on behalf of the regiment to the City. Lining the upper portion of the walls could be seen a collection of special constable's staves, used at the time of the Chartist Riots, and in adjoining cells were old fetters, manacles, gyves, a mantrap and other prison accessories, equipment of a Cromwellian trooper and a scolds bridle. This bridle was made of iron and fitted with an ingenious contrivance for gagging by means of a slip fitting well over the tongue, and was used in conjunction with a ducking stool for scolding women.

17. A picturesque ceremony of the proclamation of King George V took place throughout the land on Monday, 9th May 1910 and of all historic places in the country none could have given the ceremony a better setting than Canterbury. A vast crowd thronged the streets, with mixed feelings, the death of King Edward VII had left a note of sadness in many a heart. Dark clouds hung over the proceedings but the arrival of the 21st Lancers with tossing plumes and waving pennons brightened up the streets. The Cavalry, nearly two hundred strong, and the Buffs with fixed bayonets, lined the High Street as the Mayor and Corporation were robing in the Guildhall. Then when all was ready, the first carriage conveying the Mayor Bennett-Goldney, Brigadier General Fanshawe, the Mayor's Chaplain and Town Clerk Mr. Henry Fielding, proceeded to the corner of Guildhall Street followed by several other carriages. At the corner of the Guildhall Street, the ancient burghmote horn, a reminder of times past, was sounded three times, followed by a fanfare by the Lancer's trumpeters, then from his carriage the Town Clerk read the proclamation. The 21st Lancers mounted band then played the National Anthem after which the Mayor called in loud voice for 'Three cheers for King George V'.

18. A move was next made for the Westgate, then Northgate by the Kings School entrance, on to St. George's Gate and finally Wincheap. At each of these places the same procedure described before took place. Postcard No. 17 shows the scene at the Westgate, with the 21st Lancer's trumpeters, the Mayor waving his hat as the Town Clerk finished reading the proclamation. Also can be seen, the oldest spectators of the ceremony, Mr. and Mrs. Daley, who lived in Old Tower House, Pound Lane; and by kind thought of the police they were given an excellent position on the stone at the base of the lamp. Just in the picture are two people who had a 'bird's eye view' from the top of Barrets cycle and motor shop. This postcard shows the crowds of people in St. Peter's Street, and the scholars of Kings School and Simon Langton School who with the County Fire Brigade and Kent Fire Brigade took part in the procession. The shop in the picture recently Cornfoots the Chemists but in those days is was Maudson (late Walter Reeve) Chemist, 34 St. Peter's Street. Notices in the window announcing 'Closing Down Sale', 'The Whole Stock must be cleared', 'Sale Now On', and 'No Reasonable offer Refused'.

19. In Whitehall Road, where Toddlers Cove is today, the Canterbury Swimming Baths were opened in 1876 and being outside, they were only available from 1st June to 30th September each year. The Canterbury Swimming Club held their Annual Sports afternoon there on Thursday, 29th August 1907, when this photograph was taken. The fashions in social life were very well-illustrated at the Whitehall Baths side, when quite a few spectators turned up to see the fun. Besides the normal races, novelty events were included such as The Fifty Yard Cork Bobbing Race and Walking the Pole in fancy costume. During the afternoon there was an interesting exhibition of High and Fancy diving and the event concluded with a water polo match. During the 1920s and 1930s a familiar figure around the city with her 'Stop Me and Buy One' barrow, was Mrs. Rose Coia. You can just imagine the lucky children crowding round the ice cream lady when she visited the pool side on a hot sunny August afternoon.

View from Westgate Mill. 289.

20. At the turn of the century, when this photograph was taken, the largest single building in Canterbury, apart from the Cathedral, was Abbot's or White Mill, which stood against the eastern branch of the Stour, a few hundred yards down stream from the Black Friars monastic building. Erected in about 1824 on the site of the ancient Abbot's Mill, by John Smeaton, with a height of one hundred feet and containing six working floors plus an octagon observatory on the centre of the roof. The two water wheels which put the whole machinery into motion were sixteen feet in diameter and the mill so powerful one could not help but be impressed with the sheer size and might. The White Mill was once owned by Sidney Cooper, local artist and founder of the Art School (see card 24), the observatory at the top of the building being his studio. When repainting was in progress, on the morning of Tuesday, 17th October 1933 a fire was unintentionally started, possibly by a blow-lamp, and in a few hours the flames had reduced this magnificent building to a charred ruin. But from these ashes there has recently been built a scaled down version of the White Mill which today is used as a private residence.

21. This picture of St. Peter's Place shows the floods in the last week of October 1909. To the left can be seen the Oddfellows Arms but it is doubtful if they were busy selling Rigdens Fine Ales. Headlines in the local papers were: 'People imprisoned in their bedrooms – Punts used in streets – not for sixty years had such a flood been experienced in Canterbury.' One of the houses invaded by the water was that of Mrs. Ann Baker who would have been one hundred years old in February 1910. She lived in Black Griffin Lane, and had been bedridden for some years, and slept on the ground floor. When the floods became serious the first thought of Mr. A.J. Bond, the Relieving Officer, was of this aged lady and he at once waded through the water to reach the house. The water was just coming through the floor, but the old lady did not wish to be moved so a good fire was kept in, and fortunately, although the water rose several inches, it did not reach the fire, and the lady lived through it all.

22. Another view of the floods, this time in North Lane; the same scene would be found in Linden Grove, Ironicaly this used to be called 'Water Lane'; Westgate Grove; Pound Lane; Black Griffin Lane and Whitehall Road. In fact this part of Canterbury had become a miniature Venice. The Mayor immediately set up a Relief Fund and one of the first needs to arise was for warm food. This the Salvation Army quickly undertook to distribute from carts, which was much appreciated as can be seen in the picture. Although the Causeway cannot be seen, it is interesting to see Deans Mill, run by Mr. W. Hooker, a miller, re-named Westgate Mills in the 1930s. Sadly this was burned down in June 1954. There was a famous photograph taken of these 1909 floods called 'Water Joke' and shows the Cathedral in the background, with a complete sea of water where Sainsbury's is now. In the middle of the water there was a notice which stated 'Any persons found trespassing on the fields or damaging the fences and bridges will be prosecuted'.

23. In many ways the same scene was re-enacted again in 1927. On Boxing night householders went to bed quite unsuspecting that next morning when they awoke, the first sight that would meet their eyes downstairs, would be furniture floating in the floods which had silently invaded the lower floors. Another Appeal Fund was started by the Mayor, Alderman G.R. Barrett, as over 400 houses were flooded, £1,500 was the primary object, so a 'Souvenir Pictorial Booklet' was hurriedly published showing the devastation and hardship. A fire engine was soon at work near the Westgate Towers pumping water out of the cellars and engines from Herne Bay and Sturry had to be requisitioned to help with the task. In the picture which could be called 'All hands to the Pumps' is shown St. Peter's Restaurant and Hibble and Sons, grocers of 19 and 20 St. Peter's Street. Hand pumps and manual engines were at work throughout the day and night in an effort to cope.

T.S. Cooper's R.A. Birthplace & School of Art

24. Along the road we come to the Sidney Cooper School of Art, founded in 1867 by Thomas Sidney Cooper R.A. on the site of his own birthplace. This important institution's entrance is flanked by two Ionic columns and inside used to contain the world famous cattle painters last master piece, also his palette and brushes. Also inside was a replica in carved oak of one of the famous panels in the Hotel de Soubise in Paris which was exhibited at a Brussel's exhibition. The object of this school was to study drawing, painting and sculpture, as a part of the normal education. By 1882 Sidney Cooper was finding the strain of teaching classes of up to fifty students a little too much so he gave the building and contents to the City Council thus the Ganterbury of Art College was founded. To day the Sidney Cooper Centre retains some of its old world traditions, on a Saturday, when its doors are opened to the public to visit the weekly Antique and Craft Fair. In the postcard shown, which is dated November 1906, can also be seen part of the Crown and Sceptre Inn, Flint and Sons; W.H. Griggs, Marlow House, Picture Framer, postcard shop; and the Westgate Temperance Hotel.

St. Peter Street, Canterbury.

E 34968

CADBURY'S CHOCOL

25. The scene in this postcard of St. Peter's Street has not changed a great deal since it was postmarked in 1909. The view is from the Friars and shows Heath shops on the right (see cards 27 and 28.) It can be noted by the ruts in the street that the transformation from pedestrian, pedal and equestrian precinct into automobile roads had begun. On the left there was until fairly recently at number 51 John Field, hardware dealer. This later became Field and Jordan next door to G. Saunders, East Kent Bakery with its appetising window display and gold lettered shop front. A little further down on 3rd June 1911 opened the Canterbury Electric Theatre. The entrance was in the shape of a handsome ornamental glass canopy and at night was illuminated with miniature incandescent lights which must have provided an extremely pleasing effect. This was a leasurely era to live in with admission prices at 3d, 6d and 1s (1p, 2½p and 5 p) teas were served every afternoon, free of charge, and wait for it, at each program a speaking picture would be shown. A popular venue during the silent era, with 520 seats, the cinema closed in November 1927 when manager and staff moved over to St. Margaret's Street to take over the newly built Central Picture Theatre.

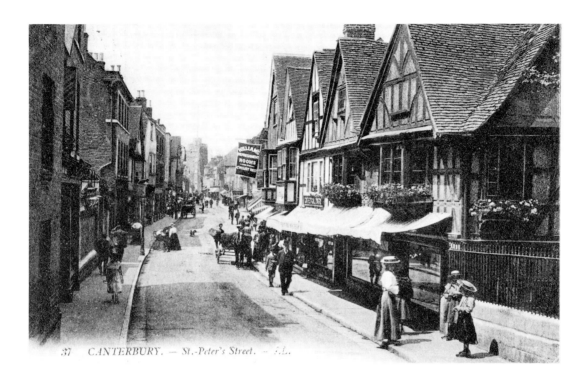

37 CANTERBURY. — St.-Peter's Street. — *L.*

26. One of the most famous and photographed views of Canterbury is shown in this picture of St. Peter's Street, taken on King's Bridge by the Weavers. Looking over the railings a very beautiful view of the downstream Stour is obtained. The gabled half-timbered, flower bedecked, water lapped houses were long occupied by the Walloon and Huguenot Refugees who settled in Canterbury and introduced the industry of weaving to the City. The Huguenots also had looms at 37 St. Peter's Street, the folding doors in the gable can still be seen, where the bales were hauled up from the street below. But back to the 'Weavers' during the 1900s the craft of hand weaving was to some extent revived in these old houses, under the proprietress of Mrs. J. Wood, visitors were admitted for 2d, to see the manufacture of Canterbury tweeds, Silk Finished Linens and Carpets on over 20 hand looms. In this postcard about 1906 can be seen the flag of Mr. Williams, Refreshment Rooms and Cyclist Restaurant at number 7a.

Compliments of the Season

1908

27. As can be seen from this truely outstanding real photographic postcard of Mr. George Heath and his wife Elsie, standing outside their two shops in St. Peter's Street, it was produced as a Christmas card for 1908. George ran the tobacconist whilst Elsie the confectionery shops at numbers 11 and 11a with Welby and Co. wine and spirit merchants (later to become the Oporto Tavern) next door. Both the shop windows were filled to capacity with Christmas goodies but the interest in this picture is the dog sitting next to Mr. Heath. Dick, the dog who liked to smoke, often took up his master's pipe from the table, in his mouth and would sit for hours with it, outside the shop. Mr. Heath had an idea and it was on 1st August 1909 (the first day of Cricket Week) that Dick took up his stool outside the shop, with his pipe between his teeth appealing for pennies for the Kent and Canterbury Hospital. Postcards were produced of Dick, to sell in the shops, showing he had collected £12.14s.4½d whilst another £28.12s.9½d in aid of the hospital funds. When the dog finally died in 1917, a special tribute was paid to him in the Kent Herald Newspaper on 21st March, which stated that Dick had collected no less than £83.7s8½d over the years.

28. Under the Motor Car Act of 1903, which came into force on 1st January 1904, all cars had to be issued with registration numbers, FN was issued for use in Canterbury. The model 'T' Ford was developed in 1908 as a relatively cheap motor car and in 1919 forty-one per cent of the motor vehicles in Britain were Fords. The model continued to be made until 1927. Another 'real gem' of photographic history is shown in this postcard of Mr. Stanley Harding standing proudly beside his model 'T' Ford. Taken in about 1924, Stan was Heath's only travelling salesman and 1930 he opened his own confectionery shop at 29 Castle Street. FN 5107 had pneumatic tyres and superb advertisements for 'Adkins Nut Brown Tobacco' on both sides. The only mention of this once flourishing business today is the painted sign high up on the back of the building which reads: 'The Friars Tuck Shop', Teas, Ices, Cigarettes and Chocolates.

29. September, 19th 1907 was a 'Red Letter Day' in the history of Canterbury General Post and Telegraph Office because on that day the Mayor Bennett-Goldney laid the foundation stone of the new General Post Office. In 1863 a Post Office was opened with a total staff of ten, at 47 St. George's Street, the names of which were placed in a bottle, buried under that foundation stone. This building functioned until lack of accommodation forced the government to look around for a larger premises. In 1868 a site and house were purchased from the late Mr. Neame, soap manufacturer of 28 High Street, and a New Post Office opened, this was further extended in 1885 to make room for the increased telephone service when it was taken over from the National Telephone Company. The new building was to be built on the site of the old Post Office and this important and impressive ceremony was attented by a large and representative gathering of citizens. The accommodation within the actual site was somewhat limited, as can be seen. Some of those present included Alderman Mason, Collard, Gentry and Stead, twelve councillors, Canon Stuart, Major Lempriere and Captain Wetherly. The builders, Mr. Shelbourne, presented the Mayor with an ivory mallot mounted in silver and suitably inscribed to perform the work on the foundation stone, which can still be seen at the front of the building today.

30. Just past the General Post Office on the corner of Stour Street, this postcard of the Benedictine Monks, who were part of the Ransomer Pilgrims, was taken in 1923 (see cards 49 and 66), as they wended their way through the city on their annual pilgrimage. To the right stands the County Hotel, dating back to the 16th century, prior to 1892 being called Ye Olde Vinter. From 1899 until 1910, when Charles Tomkins was the proprietor, their own mineral waters were made and bottled at this first class hotel. Also from the turn of the century, postcards of the hotel were given away free to guests and the hotel omnibus met all trains at the East Station. Directly opposite can be seen the Beaney Institute, with its somewhat florid half timber elevation, which was partially paid for out of a legacy left to the city by a native of Canterbury, Dr. J.D. Beany M.D. (Melbourne), who amassed a large fortune in Australia and left it to the city, to which the Council wisely added £5,000 to the original sum and had the Royal Museum and Free Library built in 1897 on the site of the old George and Dragon Inn.

Fleur-de-Lis Hotel,
CANTERBURY.

TELEPHONE 195.

THE HOSTELRIE WHERE DICKENS STAYED.

31. Continuing along the High Street from the County Hotel we come to the Fleur-de-Lis Hotel, which was the second oldest and the most interesting of the City's hostelries. Although renovated in the 1900s to provide electric lights throughout, the interior retained much of its old world character. From the courtyard, which was converted into a lounge, could be seen the 13th/14th century window, unspoiled by the restoration. In 1906 an artist P.W. Fetherstone drew the 13th century window and also a portion of a fine Tudor staircase which used to remain. These drawings plus a fine view of the outside of the hotel were issued as postcards. At about the same time the hotel still retained its livery stables although some had been converted into a motor garage to keep up with modern times. On the left of the entrance was a cosy coffee room with windows overlooking the High Street; how often must have Charles Dickens, who stayed at this hotel during his frequent visits to the City, looked out from there on the animated scene as he enjoyed a meal. Unfortunately the hotel closed in May 1955 and stayed empty for several years, the property became dilapidated and in the end was demolished, all that remains today is a plaque on the wall of the new building.

A HERNE BAY MOTOR BUS.

Photo By PEMBERTON Herne Bay.

32. The Herne Bay and East Kent Omnibus Company was formed on 14th September 1905 and in April 1906 they started a service between Canterbury and Herne Bay using a Clarkson 'Chelmsford' bus which was driven by steam with four journeys in each direction daily. A second vehicle was delivered on 10th May 1906 but the service was withdrawn for that winter on 17th November. The following summer, a very bad season, saw the company in financial difficulties and the end came on 10th November 1907; inexperienced management being the major cause of the failure. The fare was one shilling each way, between the New Dolphin Hotel, Herne Bay and the Fleur-de-Lis Hotel (see card No. 31), Canterbury, part of wich can be seen behind the bus, the other shop was Hollamby and Williams. It was in July 1891 that Mr. Hollamby and Mr. Williams opened up their gentlemen's outfitters at 35 High Street. Takings for the first week amounted to £13.12s.6d and expenses included 4s for a boy help and ls.10d for a charwoman. The hours were long, 8.30am to 8.00pm six days a week, with late nights on Friday and Saturday when the blinds were not pulled down until 10.30pm. 1923 a clothing department was added and in 1935 they moved to a larger premises at 17 St. Peter's Street.

HIGH STREET, CANTERBURY

33. This delightful evocative High Street scene of 1910 shows the grand building on the right which used to be the official headquarters of the Municipal Government of the City. Without any claim to exterior distinction in its early Victorian coat of stucco and Canterbury Coat of Arms, the Guildhall was certainly unpretentious. However, the interior possessed considerable interest, notably the Tudor Hall, which contained a number of portraits of bygone Mayors and a collection of ancient arms. Also on show were the Sword of State, being of unusual rarity and beauty, presented to the Corporation by King James I, whilst Charles II donated the Great Mace, another craftsman's art of the period. The decision to demolish this building was made and carried out, with unseemly haste, and represents the sacrifice of another object of great antiquity, likewise the Fleur-de-Lis, to the city. The reason put forward in 1951 was the cost of £18,000; today this would seem a very flimsy and scandalous excuse. To the left of the picture at 39-40 High Street was the long established firm of H.J. Goulden. They sold pianos, sheet music, stationery and produced their own excellent postcards. The street lamps outside their shop were paid for at their own expense.

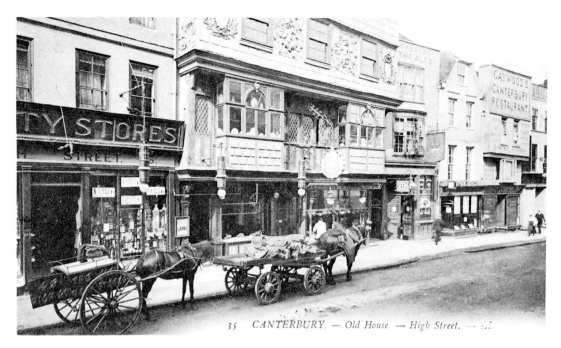

35 *CANTERBURY. — Old House. — High Street.*

34. Nearly opposite Mercery Lane in the High Street is the Queen Elizabeth's Guest Chamber, built in the 15th century by Prior Chillenden, with extensive accommodation, but it is very doubtful if Queen Elizabeth I ever stayed there. From the High Street it is very easily recognised by the highly embossed and painted figures which ornament the front of the building, but its chief claim to fame is the pargeted ceiling of the Elizabethan period, in the upper floor, described as the most perfect in the country. From the 1890s the upper part of this house was used as a gallery for the sale of antique furniture and china, trading under the sign of the 'Pilgrim's Bottel' as can be seen in the postcard. The lower part was used as shops, as it still is today, City Meat Stores and Pilcher and Chittenden, fruiterers, in the picture also are Gaywoods Restaurant, The New Crown Inn and the City Grocery Stores with their delivery horse and cart waiting for the 'off'. An advertisement from the City Stores in September 1907 reads: 'Hop Pickers, don't forget to provide yourselves with necessary refreshments. The fine health giving benefits produced by Hop Picking, can be made more permanent by the careful selection of suitable foods, such as Cooked Ham at one shilling per pound (5p), Corned Beef at sixpence per pound (2½p) and Monster Brand Milk at threepence per tin (just over 1p). City Stores the Stores for you.'

35. The building at the left of Mercery Lane used to be known as the 'Chequers of Hope Inn' and was made famous in Chaucer's Canterbury Tales. This hostelry was the favourite resting place of pilgrims but all that remains today are the pointed arches and the vaulted cellars which run the whole length of Mercery Lane. Beloved by artists the world over, retaining all its old world charm, certainly the most interesting of Canterbury's narrowest thoroughfares with Christchurch Gate and the Cathedral looming up imposingly in the distance. The sign on the left stated that Misses E. and E. Lefevre, were trading under 'Ye Olde Chequers Inn' but as ladies outfitters and now corsets specialists, not ale and porter. On the other corner where Boots is now there was T. Fox, jeweller and optician, whilst above the shop with the entrance from Mercery Lane was, and I quote from the 1912 City Guild, *stroiling along the High Street you come to one of the famous corners in the town, that of 9a Mercery Lane, now the Tea Lounge, The building with its narrow stairway and delightful low ceilinged room dated from 1550 and from its windows you can look down upon the highway trodden by in-numberable Kings and Queens.*

Mercery Lane, Canterbury

36. Mercery Lane takes its name from the circumstances that, being the direct route to the Cathedral, the shops therein sold various mementoes to the pilgrims of their visit to the sacred shrine. The delights of walking back into history are all around as you stroll down towards the Butter Market and Charles Dickens could have been talking about this lane 'with its buildings bulging out, so that it looked as if all the houses were leaning forward, trying to see who was passing on the narrow pavement below'. Passing Coast's perfumers, 'Wig and Artificial Hair Manufacturer'; Bigglestons, chemists to H.M. Queen Alexandra with displayed above their door a coat of arms, and onto J. Charlton, photographic artist's shop, the windows of which were covered in real photographic postcards. In 1893 John Charlton came to Canterbury with his wife Mary and took over Mumm's photographic shop at 54 St. George's Street where they stayed untill 1899 when a move was made to 14 Mercery Lane. He continued in business there until the end of the Second World War when ill health forced him to retire. The sad ending to this story is that when John retired over fifty years work on old glass plated negatives were dumped in the well at the back of the shop.

Old Butter Market,
Canterbury

37. The Old Butter Market was held on the site of the ancient market cross and bull stake, which the butchers of this City used to 'bait' their bulls on, in order to soften down the toughness of their flesh; the stake was removed in 1645. In 1840 a wooden building was in use, consisting of an oval roof with two lights in the centre and supported by iron columns. The market day was Saturday, when butter, poultry and eggs were brought in plenty from the neighbouring villages, but due to the bad condition of the dome this building was removed in 1888 and the Butter Market took on the appearance of our postcard from 1904. As can be seen early motor vehicles were in evidence, with porters delivery carts and the ladies besplendent in their best finery. Christchurch Gate stands majestically as the main entrance to the Cathedral, being built on that site in 1517. Though damaged by time and mutilated in 1648 this gateway still remains one of the most beautiful in the country; today the damage has been repaired. Kit Marlow's memorial can be seen, prior to being moved to the Dane John Gardens, more details of his chequered life are to be found in the foreward.

38. The traditions of the Old Butter Market were still being carried on by Clarke and Theobalds, a large provisions merchant, orders being collected and goods delivered free each week within a radius of eight miles, their premises is partly shown on the right of this picture. This was taken by Frank Bailey, photographer from Castle Street, at 2 00pm on Monday 10th October 1921 at the unveiling and dedication of the Canterbury War Memorial. The memorial was unveiled by Field Marshal Earl Haig, and those also present on the platform were the Lord Archbishop of Canterbury, The Mayor (Wright Hunt) and The Very Reverend Dean Wace. All window accommodation in the Butter Market Square was, on the suggestion of the Mayor, let at 5 shillings (25p) per head and all monies received were handed over to the Memorial Fund. Note that Warrens, the Original East Kent Clothing Mart, selected a good day to hold their 'Great Sale'.

THE MORRIS DANCERS. 1910 — M.

39. The Canterbury Carnival Society held a fete in the gardens of Ersham House, New Dover Road, on Thursday 18th August 1910, in the afternoon, when the star attractions were the Little Morris Dancers. That same evening they were in the Annual Carnival and afterwards danced in the Butter Market as can be seen in the photograph. The Morris children were trained by Mrs. Bareham (in the centre of the picture with the large hat on) and charmingly attired in white costumes with blue and yellow sashes and caps. Their delightfully executed dance movements evoked heartly applause from the watching crowds. The thirty-two boys and girls were Fanny Berge, James, Horace, Arthur, Minnie, Doris and Elsie Gomm, Mabel and Annie Austen, Horace and Dora Chandler, Lilian and Dorothy Eastman, Charles Baldock, Hilda Constant, Minnie, Dolly and Beatric Stringer, George Stickells, Billy and Dorothy Watson, Sidney and Kate Petts, Dorothy Parker, Florence Culver, Daisy Sutton, May Stewart, Ethel Baker, James and Bettie Moon, Harold David, and Mabel Cox, and lead by Viva Bareham. The shops behind the dancers were C. Wheeler, Ye Olde Cathedral Antique Rooms and Alfred Warren, outfitter and hosier, 40/41 Burgate Street.

40. Mr. Edward Neame entered the bakery trade as a young man at 20 Palace Street and by 1894 he was owner of the business. In 1901 with his brother Ted they moved to 10 Sun Street, where they baked their own bread and cakes and sold them in the shop, also opening a restaurant where roast dinners were one shilling and threepence (just over 6p). Edward's daughter Florence had to work very hard in the family business, washing up, serving in the shop and caring for the rest of the family – eight altogether. When a new law prohibited the baking of bread in ovens under shop premises, came into force, Edward Neame retired from the bakery shop and moved to Tyler Hill. The photograph was taken about 1915 and shows Hilda, one of Edward's daughters, standing in the doorway of their premises in Sun Street with the window filled to excess with culinary delights.

THE "SUN" HOTEL
(MICAWBER'S LITTLE INN),
CANTERBURY.

41. A little further on in Sun Street is 'The Little Inn', established in 1503 and where David Copperfield saw Mr. Micawber sitting at a window waiting for 'something to turn up'. At the turn of the century when this postcard view was taken the inn was still catering for the cyclist and horse-drawn passengers, the Margate four horse brakes arrived daily in the season at 1.15pm and departed at 4.00pm. The Saloon Bar had an advertisement for Redlan, Liquer Scotch Whisky, which sounds rather nice. The front part of the property was a jewellery shop owned by J. Martin, watchmaker, with displays of rings and watches, besides which plating, gilding and repairs of every description were undertaken. One of the bicycles leaning against the wall was a delivery cycle for T. Wood, pork butchers 9 Sun Street (next door to Martins) whilst the next shop was Neame's bakery (see previous card). In the distance can be made out J. Hunt and Sons, drapers, milliners, furnishers and tailors, a large departmental store in Mercery Lane where Debenham's is today. The novelty of the early photographer can be seen with the children eagerly watching and a gentleman standing to attention, ready for the camera.

42. In the Parade, nearly opposite Butchery Lane, stood the Rose Hotel. A delightful, mainly Georgian period building which for many years was the scene of much of the convivial and social life of the 'citizens', as for example when the self styled 'Knight of Malta' made this hostelry his headquarters. The postcard shown was taken in the 1920s by West of Whitstable, from the end of St. George's Street looking down the Parade. The 'Rose' which was a first class family and commercial hotel, established in 1660, now under the supervision of Miss Redman and Miss Jeans, with 'Motor Accomodation' available. This building was lost in the bombing of 1942. Directly opposite there was Taylor Brothers, corn and seed merchants, note that now the roads had been taken over by the automobile.

Royal Fountain Hotel Canterbury.

43. The most famous place in St. Margaret's Street, the Royal Fountain Hotel, used to boast it was 'the only Hotel in Canterbury patronised on many occassions by the late Queen Victoria', and over the front entrance was a large embossed Royal coat of arms. This hotel was a very old coaching inn. The Royal Mail coach used to leave from there in the 1830s at 12 00pm everyday bound for London. Ancient claims were made that the 'Fountain' was the second oldest in England, having lodged the Earl of Godwins wife in 1029 and the celebrated Archbishop Langfranc made it a temporary residence whilst his Palace at Canterbury was rebuilt in 1070. Reported also to have been used as a lodging place for the knights who murdered Becket. The end of this celebrated hostelry came in the fatal night in 1942 when it was bombed and completely gutted by fire, as was Finns Stores, which can be seen on the postcard. This was Canterbury's Edwardian 'Supermarket' where you could buy almost anything and have it delivered the same day.

Slatter's Hotel, Canterbury. Hotel Gardens.

44. The elegance of Edwardian etiquette in England could not have been better illustrated than in this picture of Canterbury. The lazy hazy days of sunny Sunday afternoons, the graceful refinement of English teas, taken under the shade of a flowering horsechestnut tree could not be pictured better anywhere else but at the Slatter's Hotel gardens. In 1900 Slatters Temperance Hotel porters met all trains, and the omnibus from the station cost 6d (2½p). This postcard was sent in August 1905 by a hotel guest; part of the message reads 'can you manage to spot me out on the otherside'. Besides Slatters Hotel with their bakers shop next door, the street used to have a Fish Market, near St. Margaret's Church (part of which is in the picture) and the Central Picture Theatre later to be transformed into the old Marlowe Theatre. Of colourful characters, Canterbury has always had its fair share but pride of place must go to Dan Sherrin, artist and practical joker. The stories of him are legionary – of sleeping in a coffin in his shop in St. Margaret's Street amongst his paintings and of 'helping' with the painting of street white lines, but into the bars of public houses.

45. The buildings on the west side of Butchery Lane have stood much as they were when this photograph was taken in 1910 and one can still enjoy the sight of Bell Harry Tower (but at this time full of wooden scaffolding) rising majestically above the roofs of the shops in Burgate Street. The eastern side of this lane is very different today due again to the bombing raids of the 1940s. Gone are the Butcher's Arms with their Rigdens Ales and Stout from Faversham, Finnis Bakery and Albert Dairy. Romance was in the air when two boys 'chatting up a girl' pushing a bicycle, stopped to watch the 'Stengel' photographer with his large brass camera record the scene. No. 1 The Parade on the corner of Butchery Lane still stands today, but it is no longer a chemist. Till 1888 Mr. D. Amos was the pharmacist, who from 1889 to 1896 went into partnership with Mr. Fowler, then in 1887 the pharmacy was taken over by Robert Croft.

Butchery Lane, Canterbury.

E 34957

The Parade, Canterbury

46. On the corner of Rose Lane along the road slightly from the Rose Hotel, was Baker's Temperance Hotel, 31 St. George's Street. This family and commercial hotel was established in 1874 and when this photograph was taken in 1904 Mr. Alfred G. Baker was the proprietor. The building itself dated back to Tudor times and in one of the rooms there was a shield over the door bearing 'Anno Domini 1632', sadly this was another property to be destroyed in the June Blitz 1942 as was the Corn Exchange on the opposite side of the road. The Corn Exchange was erected in 1824, on the site of the old shambles, in the fashionable neoclassical style with three openings to the fruit and vegetable market, on the site where the Longmarket is now. Also in the front of the building were the arms of the city, flowers in abundance and on Saturdays wide passageways lined with stalls selling flowers, vegetables, meat, second hand furniture, books and bric-a-brac.

47. A car was a valuable asset in Canterbury on polling day during the General Election of 15th January 1910 between Sir John Henniker Heaton (Conservative), Mr. F. Bennett-Goldney (Independent Unionist) and Mr. Drysdale Woodcock (Liberal). Many people still felt that the car was a toy of the rich, but all parties used cars extensively to take voters to the polls. The photograph shows Mr. and Mrs. Woodcock in their decorated car outside their committee rooms at 10 The Parade with another Woodcock supporters car behind them. There was a very high turn out for this election, due possibly to the car transporting people to the polling stations. Out of 3,957 Canterbury electors, 3,536 people voted but despite all his hard work Drysdale Woodcock came third with 815 votes; Bennett-Goldney 1,350; and Henniker Heaton 1,371; a very close thing. In December of the same year another General Election took place, this time Bennett-Goldney standing as Independent candidate proved successful.

48. On 1st June 1942 nearly all the buildings in St. George's Street were raised to the ground in the 'Baedeker' raid and thus this view showing the whole length of the street is today unrecognisable, except for the St. George's Clock which can just be made out at the top of the picture. Architecturally the street was something of a medley and as shown the buildings were predominately plain although a few had character and age. To the left of the street can be seen the Maypole Dairy, with an advert for their tea, Biggleston H.M. and Sons, Ironmongers, Nash's East Kent Brush Co and the World Stores. The procession walking along the narrow roadway was the annual pilgrimage by members of the Guild of our Lady of Ransom led by the Reverend Dr. Amigo, the Bishop of Southwark. After a service in the Roman Catholic Church the procession visited the scene of the Martyrdom in the Cathedral (see cards 30 and 66).

36 CANTERBURY. — St. George's Street.

49. The changes in St. George's Street can be more easily placed in this 1907 view taken from what is now the roundabout at the top of the town. Everything failed to survive the bombing except the Tower of St. George's Church which now forms the centre piece of a modern shopping precinct, linking the ancient and modern together. On the back of this card is a detailed report of a Kent and Yorkshire cricket match at the end of the 1907 season, part of which reads: 'Kent had a bad time later on and had to stonewall for their lives, maiden over after over.' In the end Kent managed to draw the match. The demon bowler Colin Blythe was playing for Kent but there was no mention of Frank Woolley who was enjoying his first full season for the county. The large departmental store on the corner was F.W. Martin, draper, silk merchant, costumier and ladies outfitters, whilst opposite stood the premises of Mr. Pollard, the jeweller, who carried on his business in what had originated as a timber framed house, the front of which he opened up and restored.

50. This is a most unusual view showing the tops of the buildings of St. George's Gate, taken in 1908 from a chimney stack which was at the rear of 5 Dover Street. Part of the message reads: '...this was taken from the scaffold round the chimney. Tell Lorna to see if she can see Old Ginger, Doctor Prentice's horse, looking out of his stable door, in the right hand corner.' Doctor Prentice's horse must have been kept at George Crow's livery stables, 11 Lower Bridge Street, later to become the site of St. George's Theatre, opened by the Mayor Ald. F.J. Godden on 8th February 1915. A sound system was installed in 1930 to allow the presentation of the new 'talkies'. However, the arrival of two new super cinemas in 1933 led to the desertion of its patrons and shows ceased in May 1934. The buildings shown in St. George's Gate were: 4, B. & W. Fisk Moore, photographer; 3, A.T. Bates, gun cycle and motor department; 2, F.J. Deveries, Pianoforte dealer and tuner; 1. S.B. Pettitt, stationers. The Cathedral with its wooden scaffolding looks very similar to card number 46, which is a common place sight even today but the large GPO telegraph pole with its 'eight way arms', filled with white insulators and finial on the top of the pole, are just a memory of the past, as are the buildings.

34   CANTERBURY. — The Market. — ...

51. It may truly be said of Canterbury that it is the centre of the 'Garden of England', as the County of Kent is so practically described. Some of the most charming orchards and hop fields can be seen in the immediate neighbourhood and on Market Days everyone seems to flock into the City. The Cattle Market was held between the City Wall and Upper Bridge Street, running from the Riding Gate to St. George's Gate. That confined space was a hive of activity, with people like Betsy Trotwood, 'insinuating her grey pony among the carts, baskets, vegetables and huckster's goods' generally with a gallery audience overlooking from St. George's Terrace. This postcard, published at the turn of the century, shows the market in full flood. The auctioneers had their offices built into the city wall with names such as Messrs. Marchant; Petley; Finn; King and Ashenden.

52. Strings of horses, herds of cattle, flocks of sheep, with occasional droves of pigs, were driven through the City streets to and from the market. For anything to be transported was an exception rather than the rule. The market folk came from all walks of life and this weekly get together was a 'gathering of the clans', many were real characters, none more so than the drovers. Market days were always colourful and hectic especially after the cattle drivers, a good humoured crowd, had paid several visits to the 'Beehive' or the 'Flying Horse' public houses. This postcard from about 1910 shows some fine Shire horses with their tails being plaited prior to the auction, with a goodly audience watching from the St. George's Terrace above. The horse trough which now stands beside the Westgate Towers was first placed in the cattle market.

53. The Salvation Army commands a public respect and over the years the Army's work with the down and outs, the elderly, the poor, and in war areas, has proved the value of practical Christianity. This year the Canterbury Salvationists celebrate their centenary being established in 1886 but this postcard, taken by Frank Bailey, dated from about 1920. During the summer months the Salvation Army held open air services on a Sunday afternoon at the Cattle Market, after which they would march down St. George's Street and The Parade to the Citadel in White Horse Lane, singing hymns, accompanied by their brass band, for the evening service. Salvationists mingled with the crowds, tambourines and their traditional bonnets making them look very smart; the colour sergeant Mr. Branchard had a wooden leg, but this did not prevent him from joining the parade. Today the Georgian terrace has disappeared and the bus station taken its place, whilst the Cattle Market is now just part of the ring road but tradition still continues every Monday at a new venue appropriately named Market Way.

54. Sunday 15th October 1922 was a proud and sad day for the Royal East Kent Yeomanry, for that day recorded the last appearance of the regiment and the unveiling of their War Memorial by Lord Harris, a former Colonel. Thousands of people thronged the streets as the Yeomanry, past and present, assembled outside the Drill Hall in St. Peter's Lane. Massed bands of the Buffs headed the column as they marched off, followed by Yeoman carrying regimental wreaths, to the Cathedral where in the precincts the Mayor, Wright Hunt, took the salute. After a service, the regiment reformed and marched to the site of the Memorial at St. George's Gate, police and special constables had to join hands to keep the crowds back enabling the troops to march through. St. George's Terrace was reserved for relatives of the fallen and surviving elderly Yeomen. After the 'last post' stirringly sounded by the trumpeters of the 10th Royal Hussars and the 'unveiling', floral tribes were placed around the memorial, red and green predominated, being the regimental colours. The memorial took the form of an Ionic column surmounted by an urn and flames with cartouches attached to the column of the regimental badge and motto, in the background can be seen part of Upper Bridge Street including St. George's Garage and the Ministry of Labour and Employment Exchange. In recent years to facilitate the building of the ring road the memorial was transferred to a new site outside Nason's in the High Street.

55. In many ways Burgate Street suffered but not so severely from enemy action during that June raid and surprisingly many of the buildings survived. The photograph shown was taken in the 1920s from the Lower Bridge Street end, looking towards Sun Street, with the Ransomer Pilgrims making their way towards the Tower of St. Mary Magdalene and then into the Church of St. Thomas. At the top of Burgate stood the brewery of George Beer, outside the city wall, with Bate's garage sharing the corner with the Old Saracen's Head, public house, further down was the Crown Inn; all these buildings are no longer with us. The blind of Court Brothers can be made out in the picture, that building and all subsequent houses are still standing but not so of Geeson's White House and the Co-op. Geeson's cash clothier was for many years on the corner of Butchery Lane until moving to 21B, the White House. This was just the shop to buy trousers at 4slld (25p) a pair or a light flannel suit for the hot summer days at 18s6d (82½p).

56. Standing on the corner of Church Street, St. Paul's at 1 Broad Street, there was always a butchers shop. In 1890 it was owned by Mr. T. Horne and Son but by 1897 it had been taken over by William Horne, probably the son. Mr. R.H. White bought the business in about 1909 and then in 1912 he sold the butchery shop to William Boorman, who carried on the tradition of the shop being a family butchers. An advertisement in 1902 stated that the butchery specialised in 'Prime Pickled Tongues and Southdown Mutton' and that 'Whole families were supplied on reasonable terms'. Animals were purchased at the market, only a stone's throw away, and with their own slaughter house behind the shop, meat could not have been fresher. The photograph was taken in December 1913, with the shop laden with Christmas specials, a wonderful display of meat and Mr. Boorman standing by the door, clad in his butcher's apron, knife and steel at the ready. The two assistants, come delivery boys, were standing with their butchers bikes, wicker baskets loaded with orders, ready for a wet ride around the city streets. W. Boorman's shop was another victim of the blitz, but in true British tradition the business carried on in temporary accommodation at 9 Longport Street, William's private house.

57. One of the most extraordinary occurences happened at Church Street, St. Paul's on 26th July 1905, the front wall of the upper part of a house just 'fell out'. The dwelling was a two storey tenement occupied, at this time, by Miss Bartholomew, a dressmaker, and owned by Mr. Rogers, the baker next door. The occupant had heard ominous crackings and spoke to the landlord but after inspection he concluded that there was no immediate danger. Then in the early hours of that morning the whole of the upper part of the outer wall crashed down, ceiling as well, but luckily Miss Bartholomew was unhurt. As soon as the occurrence became known there were a large number of sight-seers on the spot, among them were a few of the local photographers anxious to record the spectacle.

58. A plaque on the railings outside the St. Augustine's Abbey Gardens is all that is left of the Kent and Canterbury Hospital which once stood on this land. This real photographic postcard published by Mr. A.A. Noakes of St. Peter's Street was posted in May 1906 and as can be seen the hospital was established in 1793. In 1904 the annual expenditure for the Longport Hospital was £4,000 and this was supported only by voluntary subscriptions, people like 'Dick the Dog who liked to smoke' (see card 27). There were 106 beds for patients and during that year the physicians and surgeons dealt with 818 in-patients and 1,082 out-patients. The hospital steadfastly served the sick and poor until 1937, but most people will remember the building's use as the Canterbury Technical School and College until it was pulled down in 1977.

59. Over the years a controversy has existed in Canterbury about the actual address of Uriah Heep's 'umble ome' of Charles Dickens fame. One official guide book of this City from the turn of the century mentions it was in North Lane whilst another favours Lower Chantry Lane. There was a notice in the wall of one of a row of cottages in Lower Chantry Lane stating that Uriap Heep lived there. The photograph shown here is of the lane and cottages, 'umble ome' being No. 4, these cottages were demolished in the 1942 blitz and now the Safeways store stands on this site. The other building in North Lane was on the site now used as a car park, but pre-war there was a placard in the window, calling it the 'umble ome'. In David Copperfield, Uriah had originally lived with his mother but when David returned to Canterbury, after becoming engaged to Dora, Uriah and his mother had moved and were living with Mr. Wickfield. Could this be the end of the mystery? Who knows!

60. The Invicta locomotive was built by George Stephenson in 1821 and was used on the Canterbury to Whitstable Railway, until 1838. Through the concern of Mr. F. Bennett-Goldney, this historic engine now appropriately finds a last resting place in Canterbury. This was the generous gift of Sir David Solomans, Bart., of Broomhill, who during the 1890s saved it from destruction when the directors of the Railway Company proposed to relegate it to the scrap heap. The Invicta arrived in the city on 7th June 1906 and was positioned near the Riding Gate, on the outside of the City walls. The photograph shows the scene, a hot sunny afternoon, on Wednesday 8th August 1906, with Sir David unveiling the engine. Those present also included the Mayor, Bennett-Goldney, Deputy Mayor Anderson, Aldermen Gentry, Hart, Stead, Sheriff Wood and Councillors. Two years later the Invicta was one of the star attractions at the Franco-British Exhibition held in London and then it was back to the Riding Gate site until 1969 when she was moved to a new home in the Dane John Gardens, because of the new ring road. Today however, it is now undercover, having been restored, and can be seen at the Poor Priests Hospital Museum in Stour Street.

61. Throughout East Kent on 19th July 1919 there was a very full programme of festivities arranged including childrens sports, firework displays and the chain of beacon bonfires, all to celebrate the 'Great Peace Day'. The events arranged in Canterbury were fairly numerous, with the military giving valuable help to the 'Council Peace Celebration Committee'. The major event commenced at noon with a procession by the Mayor and Corporation from the Guildhall to the Dane John Moat to officially receive the tank from Major General Sir Colin Mackenzie. The tank which had been placed in the moat the previous day, was presented by the National War Savings Committee in recognition of the City's financial assistance, nearly £250,000 given during the war. In the photograph taken from the Dane John Terrace by John G. Charlton can be seen the Mayor and Mayoress Bremner, Sheriff Pentecost and Aldermen Pope and Wiltshire. This picturesque ceremony was watched with obvious interest by some thousands of citizens assembled on the upper Dane John Terrace, in the Rhodaus Town thoroughfare and in the moat itself. A guard of honour was formed by fifty soldiers from the Buffs, bearing their decorated lances, whilst a guard was also provided by a contingent from the 5th Royal Irish Lancers. The band of the 1st Battalion the Buffs was also in attendance.

Entrance, Dane John, Canterbury.

62. For this years Cricket Week, 1907, Dane John Entrances were more tastefully decorated than usual with illuminations and pretty baskets of flowers. When the French Gymnasts visited the city earlier in the year (see card 64) the council voted for a new entrance gate to be built in the Watling Street end of the Dane John Gardens. An ornate and splendid wrought iron gate was constructed with 'Welcome' standing out proudly in electric 'fairy' lights, over the top, this cost the council £21.13s6d (£21.67½p) to provide. Whilst at the Watling Street entrance the 'Welcome' stood out prominently, the whole gardens were not overshadowed, being bedecked, like a fairy paradise, with small coloured glass illumination lamps, each with a night light inside, glowing and twinkling in the twilight, from the flower beds and in the trees. The fountain looked exceedingly pretty with strings of couloured lights stretched from the base to the summit, giving an array of brilliant colours, reflecting into the water beneath.

Dane John, Canterbury

63. In the evenings during part of the summer time and every evening during 'Cricket Week' the Dane John Bandstand was brilliantly illuminated with varicoloured lights, for the concerts from 8.00pm until 10.00pm and through the 'Welcome' entrance the crowds thronged. The Dane John open air concerts were always very well-attended and the demand for seats was usually far in excess of the supply, unless the weather prevented all but the brave from turning up. It was nothing to see crowds numbering over one thousand in attendance to listen to the excellent programmes and feasts of music, which were always highly appreciated. The city's military could always be relied upon to play in the bandstand; in 1910 the 21st Lancers Band and in 1905 the 7th Dragoon Guards. The Canterbury City Silver Band also made regular appearances as did Mr. W.T. Harvey's Orchestra. During the 1920s at the St. George's Picture Theatre, near the cattle market, the orchestra was under the direction of W.T. Harvey, A.R.C.O.

64. On Tuesday 2nd July 1907, 900 members of the 'Calais Congress of the Association Regionale of the Union of Gymnastic Society', came to Canterbury for the day. The party consisted of 500 French Gymnasts, 250 Congress Members and two bands. They came over on a special steamer Calais-Folkestone and then a special train to Canterbury West Station, arriving at 10.30am. Having been received in state at the Westgate, the Gymnasts marched in procession to the Cathedral for a short service. Next to the Corn Exchange for a public luncheon and then onto the St. Lawrence Cricket Ground for a gymnastic display. The postcard shows the band of the 1st Battalion of the Buffs followed by flag bearers of the gymnasts in procession along Rhodaus Town, with the Dane John to the right and in the distance the approach to Canterbury East Station and Godden's furniture depository. That evening there was quite a feast of music in the Dane John Gardens with the two french bands and the Buffs each giving performances. At the Watling Street entrance to these lovely gardens a pretty arrangement of electric lights, bidding the visitors 'Welcome', had been especially provided (see card 62) whilst the bandstand was brilliantly illuminated with red and white lights.

65. This fascinating glimpse from the past shows just how much this part of Canterbury has changed. The 1910 scene is another of the announcement venues of the succession to the throne of King George V staged on 9th May (see also cards 17 and 18 for the Proclamation details). The picture was taken from what is now Wincheap roundabout, facing towards Canterbury East Railway Station and shows the Station Hotel, Presbyterian Church, Castle Inn and the Man of Kent (then the Railway Hotel). Obviously most of the transport was horse-drawn, but an early motor car can be seen in Station Road and an outside porters barrow, familiar to those days, is drawn up by the kerb. The band and escorts were the 21st Lancers, then stationed at Canterbury. Mr. C. Skam, fly proprietor of Oaten Hill, provided the carriages, the drivers must have been familiar figures around the Canterbury streets.

66. The annual pilgrimage in July 1910 by members of the Guild of our Lady of Ransom was rather larger than usual. No less than one hundred and sixty adherents from London arrived at Canterbury East Station at about noon to be joined by contingents from Hastings, Thanet and East Kent. Among the orders represented were Benedictines, Carmelites, Passionists and Jesuits. The visitors were met by the Reverend E. Shepherd and his choir boys and then singing the pilgrimage hymns the picturesque procession wended its way via the Dane John and streets of Canterbury to St. Thomas' Roman Catholic Church. The pilgrims were welcomed at the Catholic Church by the Bishop of Southwark, The Right Reverend Dr. Amigo and the Litanes of the Saints were sung. After venerating the relics of St. Thomas in its beant casket, they were carried immediately in front of Dr. Amigo as the pilgrimage visited the scene of the Martyrdom in Canterbury Cathedral which was followed by a service. The scene shown here was taken from St. Andrew's Presbyterian Church, showing the young converts walking from the Castle Hotel along Wincheap Green towards the Dane John (see also cards 30 and 49).

67. In the early 1920s when this photograph was taken, the road surfaces were in a deplorable condition, passing vehicles would splash mud over any passer by and also give the shop windows a coating. A vast improvement came about when the main streets were closed for weeks while the contractors Messrs. Chittenden and Simmonds carried out a major project. Possibly this was due to the election of Mr. G.R. Barrett to the council, as his election slogan ran: 'If you would turn this pot hole City into a top hole City Vote for George Barrett.' At about the same time the East Kent Bus Company ran two city services; Whitstable Road to St. Lawrence Road and The Hop Poles to Sturry Road; with a fare on either of 1½d (½p) all the way. Also outside the Hop Poles public house in Wincheap is shown Ash's delivery horse and cart, stacked with 'Canterbury Ales, Stouts and Porter' in casks and bottles. On the right is Bert Fagg, a draymen. Ash's brewery was sited on what is a now a car park, in St. John's Lane next to the Dane John Gardens.

68. Life at the turn of the century generally moved at a far slower pace, more than half the trade and private vehicles were horse-drawn, including contractors and carrier's vans. Traction and other steam engines were still in full use, although internal conbustion engines, powered by petrol, were gradually taking over. Brett's and Finn's traction engines plied their trade per hour, drawing three trucks laden with stone plus a water barrel. Somewhat faster were the Foden engines and Clayton undertypes which both Messrs. Brett and Yeoman used and early each morning George Yeoman, one of three brothers (Charles, George and Walter) could be seen carrying out early inspections outside their premises at 1 Wincheap Street, to ensure all was well with the vehicles. The photograph was taken outside the Water Works in Wincheap Street about 1920 and shows one of their fleet of Dennis delivery lorries. Commercial vehicles continued to use solid tyres for years after cars had pneumatic, mainly because manufacturers and users doubted whether tubes would stand up to heavy commercial wear and tear.

69. To stimulate trade and provide maximum employment locally in 1920 the **Canterbury and District Chamber of Trade** initiated a 'Shopping Week' and so successful was it that in 1922 it was revived. Free shopping guides were printed and distributed to all households, friendly rivalry existed among the traders; special competition window displays were arranged; there were free gifts for shoppers studying the windows and this was not just for the High Street area but also included Wincheap. This picture taken by local photographer Chambers of Wincheap, shows his street with Bell Harry Tower just visible in the distance. The gas street lighting and the cycle shop are the only things to have disappeared. With the headquarters of the Canterbury Cycle Club only just around the corner, Mr. P. Forwood's Cycle Engineering Works would have done a brisk trade in repairs. Horse-drawn transport of all kinds was used by bakers, milkmen and other trades, the owner of one of these can be seen passing the time of day with a friend, whilst on the opposite side of the road, with the blind pulled down, was Wincheap Post Office and grocers run by George Harris.

70. Cycling was a popular hobby with the late Victorians and Edwardians and by the 1890s, with the invention of the lady's safety bicycle (wheels of equal diameter), it enabled women to join this sport which had previously been a male preserve. Penny farthings were superseded by these new models and multiseat cycles enjoyed a brief popularity, some were built to seat up to seven people but proved very cumbersome to handle. Cycling as a recreation perhaps reached its apogee in the twenties when cycling clubs proliferated, the Cyclist's Touring Club was founded in 1910, with their CTC advertising signs becoming prominent on many buildings and even a National Cyclist's Union was started. In 1909 the Canterbury Cycling Club was so popular that when a picnic run to Perry Woods was arranged they had to hire two large horse brakes from S.M. Burton, St. George's livery stables to transport all their non-cycling supporters. The photograph was taken outside the clubs headquarters, The Imperial public house, Martyrs Field Road, and in the background can be seen the city's gasometer. Other club events for that year included a midnight cycle run to Tunbridge Wells, in the rain; a twenty-five mile team road race against Margate Cycling Club, and a run out to Denton for a Church parade.

71. To most people the Church Army is looked upon for its valuable voluntary welfare work, maintaining soup canteens, helping the elderly, the down and outs and social care, but this is only part of their work. The Reverend Prebendary Wilson Carlile founded the Church Army in 1882 and was their leader for sixty years. The training for an evangelist lasted eighteen months and included a mixture of study and practical experience in field work. The photograph, which was taken in the 1930s, shows two Church Army Captains standing outside their field mission caravan for the Canterbury Area. As this is number one caravan, there must have been at least two travelling in this area, working to a very strict disciplined programme of devotion preaching, door to door visitations and holding short open air Gospel meetings. Guilt lettering, spreading the word of the Lord, skilfully decorated this Burton type wagon with panelled body and unmistakable domed roof, with possibly a clerestory in the roof, to improve the headroom when the Captains were not outside expressing the Christian faith.

72. The custom of 'Beating the Bounds' is not one which is peculiar only to Canterbury, for years ago the official representatives of old established towns and villages were in the habit of periodically inspecting the boundaries of their areas. The present boundaries were, according to reliable tradition, defined in the time of Archbishop Theodore, but the date when this historic custom was established cannot be ascertained. 1887, 1894 and 1903 were the last recorded events, when plenty of fun, frivolity and horseplay went into the days proceedings. Monday 26th September 1910 was the date of the next beating ceremony and at nine o'clock in the morning between seventy and eighty people assembled at St. Stephen's level crossing, armed with their 'willow wands' ready for the walk. The Mayor Bennett-Goldney and Alderman Gentry were ceremoniously bumped on the first boundary stone, whilst other members of the party touched the marker stone with their willow sticks. During the days walk other people would take their turn at being 'bumped'.

73. Card No. 72 dated from 1910 was taken during a refreshment break at Mr. Lilleywhite's yard in Hollow Lane. In the picture can be seen 'Tubby' Lilleywhite, Ledger with the bowler hat (on left), Bennett-Goldney, with long scarf Fisk-Moore and J. Charlton, both armed with semi-portable plate cameras, strange as it may seem there was only one lady in the party, a Miss Francis. On closer inspection of the picture it can be seen that several people are holding M.A. Robins' of Broad Street, stone ginger beer bottles, whilst the majority are drinking Canterbury Ales. The other photograph is taken from the next 'Beating of the Bounds' ceremony which took place on 26th September 1919, recorded by local photographer Frank Bailey from Castle Street. The view is of St. Stephen's railway crossing, in the distance can be seen railway signals and to the left, part of Mackinson's Malt House. Councillor Stone, 'Stoney' to his friends, town sergeant Jarvis and town crier Lilley are wearing their pictuesque cocked hats and gold braided uniforms, also two dogs are 'smelling' the C.C.C. boundary stone. This event really went down in history because the proceedings were filmed for Gaumont Graphic and Pathe News.

Earl Roberts visit to Canterbury — Aug 26th 1902

The appearance much agrees along will suit splendidly

74. For grateful acknowledgement of eminent services rendered to the Empire, Field Marshal Earl Roberts and General Sir John French were honoured at Canterbury on 26th August 1902 by being presented with the Freedom of the City. Arriving at Canterbury West Station via the Ostend Boat Express, they mounted horses and rode to the Canterbury Barracks, taking in a grand tour of the city en-route. The presentation was officially made at a ceremony in the Guildhall after which lunch was held at the County Hotel. This picture is a very early photographic real postcard of Earl Roberts and General French on their visit to Canterbury. The photograph was taken from opposite No. 1 Military road, which was the property of Frederick T. Gentry, builder, decorator and undertaker, and was posted on 22nd September 1902.

75. From the early 1900s a number of small motor omnibus concerns were operating in the eastern part of Kent. The roads were often unsuitable for heavy transport, the vehicles were unreliable with heavy maintenance costs and financial backing was hard to find. The advent of the war multiplied the difficulties; it was not long before several operators in East Kent realised that in order to survive they must pool their resources and as a result in August 1916 the East Kent Road Car Company was formed. The old Canterbury Bus Station was in St. Peter's Place and the photograph shows a Tilling Stevens TS6, petrol, electric, East Kent Bus on the Canterbury to Ashford route. FN5541, new in 1923, was the first bus to use an enclosed drivers compartment. The photograph was taken outside the Woolpack Inn, Chilham, prior to 1930 when the bus was withdrawn from passenger service and sold; on the left stands the conductor, Bert Relf, and to his right the driver, Charles Rowe.

"CANTERBURY UNDER FIRE" GENERAL VIEW

86775

76. Canterbury was in the front line of Britain during the Second World War and suffered considerable damage from enemy action, as has been mentioned several times in this book. The destruction wrought by the 'Baedeker Raid' on the night of 1st June 1942 decimated the St. George's Street area, Burgate, Butchery Lane, Rose Lane, Watling Street, Lady Woottons Green and many other parts of the city were also heavily damaged, but still the main part of the Cathedral stood. Hundreds and hundreds of incendiary bombs were dropped on the city and fierce fires swept through the streets, the glare, providing an awe inspiring spectacle for miles around. Although not in the period covered by this book, this picture, having been passed by the censor, was taken from the Cathedral soon after the blitz and shows the remains of St. George's Street, Burgate and Longmarket areas. As a result of the war, today the shopping centre has achieved a new look, modern designed buildings have obliterated the former scars of war, so that in effect an ancient city and a new town stand cheek by jowl. 'Ave Mater Angliae' Hail Mother of England.